To all SEUSA employees:

On behalf of Suncor Energy's board of directors and the executive committee, I want to personally thank you for your contribution to the company's success in 2007.

It was a busy and challenging year and I appreciate your dedication to the business. In true Suncor spirit, everyone worked as a team to meet the challenges and achieve one of the highest scores for the Annual Incentive that Suncor has seen.

Given that the U.S. refining and marketing business is the newest addition to the Suncor family, I am very proud of this accomplishment. You can be very proud, as well.

I hope you enjoy this book about Colorado as a commemoration of this achievement.

Sincerely,

Rick George
President & CEO

Our Colorado

Text and Photography by J. C. Leacock

Voyageur Press

First published in 2003 by Voyageur Press, an imprint of MBI Publishing Company, Galtier Plaza, Suite 200, 380 Jackson Street, St. Paul, MN 55101-3885 USA

MBI Publishing Company titles are also available at discounts in bulk quantity for industrial or sales-promotional use. For details write to Special Sales Manager at MBI Publishing Company, Galtier Plaza, Suite 200, 380 Jackson Street, St. Paul, MN 55101 USA.

To find out more about our books, join us online at www.VoyageurPress.com

Library of Congress Cataloging-in-Publication Data

Leacock, J. C.
  Our Colorado / text and photography by J. C. Leacock.
    p. cm.
  ISBN-13 978-0-89658-549-2
  1. Colorado—Pictorial works. 2. Landscape—Colorado—Pictorial
rial
works. 3. Colorado—Description and travel. I. Title.
  F777.L435 2003
  978.8'002—dc21
                    2003012687

Printed in Hong Kong

Page 1: *Capitol Peak, located in White River National Forest, towers to a majestic 14,130 feet.*

Page 2: *Aspen trees and buffalo berry color the forest in autumn.*

Page 3: *The North Fork Boulder Creek cascades over a rocky ledge just outside of Boulder, in Roosevelt National Forest.*

Page 4: *Long ago, Ancestral Pueblo Peoples inhabited Tower Point Ruin, part of the Horseshoe group of Puebloan-era ruins in Hovenweep National Monument, near the Utah border.*

Page 5: *The evening sun warms the colorful buildings that line Silverton's main street.*

Title page: *A Lodgepole fence near Ridgeway appears to mirror the Dallas Divide in the distance.*

Title page, inset: *This old store in St. Elmo, near Buena Vista, is part of one of the best preserved ghost towns in the state.*

Facing page: *Independence Monument seems aptly named on this morning in Colorado National Monument.*

Top: *On the pristine grounds of Bent's Old Fort National Historic Site, saltgrass basks in the rich morning light.*

Above: *Highway 109 seems to go on forever as it passes through Comanche National Grasslands on Colorado's southeastern plains.*

Right: *In an endless sea of prairie, Pawnee Buttes, now part of Pawnee National Grasslands, were a landmark for westward-bound pioneers.*

Facing page: *National Park Service employee and re-enactor Bob Kisthart, dressed as the fort hunter, provides visitors with a glimpse of what life might have been like at Bent's Old Fort in the 1830s.*

Left and below: *In the 1830s, Bent's Old Fort was the only trading post along the Santa Fe Trail, and a popular stopping place for beaver-trapping mountain men, Native Americans, and the U.S. Army. Today, Bent's Old Fort is a National Historic Site.*

Top: *The Linden Hotel (c.1883) is a well-known landmark in Fort Collins's historic Old Town.*

Right: *Students bike to class along the Oval at Colorado State University in Fort Collins.*

Facing page: *Sturdy elm trees shade the walkway to the Colorado State University Administration Building. The university is internationally recognized for its school of veterinary medicine.*

Right: *Dew covers a spider web in Moraine Park, Rocky Mountain National Park.*

Below: *The Big Thompson River winds through the tall meadow grasses of Moraine Park, Rocky Mountain National Park.*

Facing page: *Indian Peaks Wilderness is perhaps the most visited of all wilderness areas in Colorado, and Brainard Lake, seen here at sunrise, is one of the more popular entry points.*

At an elevation of 14,225 feet, Long's Peak is climbed more often than any of Colorado's other fifty-three "fourteeners." Long's Peak is pictured at sunset, near Rock Cut, Trail Ridge Road, Rocky Mountain National Park.

Top: *As the short summer season begins in the highcountry, ice breaks up and melts in Blue Lake, Indian Peaks Wilderness.*

Above: *Ice melting from the surface of a high-altitude lake is a harbinger of summer.*

Left: *Hallet Peak reflects in the morning stillness of Sprague Lake, Rocky Mountain National Park.*

Above: *In Colorado, wildlife is so abundant it appears in some unexpected places. Here an Elk grazes on the golf course in Estes Park. Photograph © Erwin & Peggy Bauer*

Above: *Over the years, the water flowing over Chasm Falls has eroded away the rock to form this tiny canyon in Rocky Mountain National Park.*

Facing page: *Sometimes nature is the artist. Aspen leaves are arranged serendipitously on a lichen-covered rock, San Juan Mountains.*

Facing page: *Old-Man-of-the-Mountain wildflowers bloom on a ridge overlooking Forest Canyon, Rocky Mountain National Park.*

Left: *A backpacker sets off for the weekend from Brainard Lake in Indian Peaks.*

Below: *A grove of aspens crowd an old mining cabin in Hessie Townsite (ghost town), Roosevelt National Forest.*

Top: *A backcountry skier makes his way to a Tennessee Mountain cabin in Roosevelt National Forest, one of many cabins and huts available to backcountry explorers in the Rockies.*

Above: *Bear Lake seems to sleep in the early winter mist, Rocky Mountain National Park.*

Right: *James Peak, the centerpiece of James Peak Wilderness, designated in 2002, assumes a pink glow during a winter sunrise.*

Ore carts were once the workhorses of the Argo Gold Mine and Mill, Idaho Springs.

Left: *The historic Goldminer Hotel in the old mining town of Eldora has been in business since the early 1900s.*

Below: *Mailboxes line the road in the quiet mountain community of Eldora.*

Above: *Students at the University of Colorado at Boulder enjoy a spring day on the lawn of the Quadrangle in front of Norlin Library. The library, built around 1939, is named after George Norlin, who was president of the university in the early 1900s.*

Right: *Musicians entertain passersby on Pearl Street Mall.*

Facing page: *Bookends is but one of the many casual cafes that line Boulder's Pearl Street Mall.*

Facing page: *The Flatirons, which are within view from just about everywhere in Boulder, are the town's signature backdrop.*

Above: *Opened in 1898 as part of the nationwide cultural "Chautauqua" movement, the Chautauqua Dining Hall beneath Boulder's Flatirons still serves patrons to this day.*

Left: *A climber scales the North Cut in Eldorado Canyon State Park, near Boulder.*

Above: *Since its humble beginnings as a tiny mining camp in 1859, Denver has grown to be the largest metropolis in the Mountain West.*

Facing page: *Built in 1892, The Brown Palace Hotel in downtown Denver has been host to numerous presidents, royalty, international dignitaries, and celebrities throughout its history.*

Left: *A whimsical light display transforms the Denver City and County Building during the holiday season. The building, completed in 1932, is the centerpiece of Denver's Civic Center Park.*

Above: *A statue of a bronc rider, a fitting symbol of the American West, stands tall in downtown Denver's Civic Center Park.*

The Navarre Building is surrounded by modern skyscrapers in downtown Denver. The building was home to the Joseph Brinker Collegiate Institute for Young Women in the 1880s, and it has been carefully renovated.

Above: *City Park Pavillion and the Denver skyline reflect in Ferril Lake at City Park, Denver.*

Left: *Larimer Street, once within Denver's skid row, is now a vibrant part of Lower Downtown.*

Overleaf: *Rock formations glow in the morning light at Garden of the Gods Park, located just minutes from downtown Colorado Springs.*

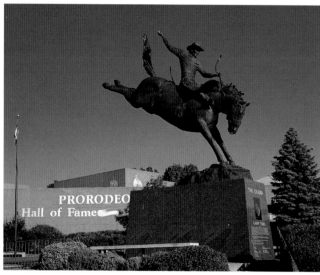

Top: *A five-star luxury hotel with lots of style, The Broadmoor, has long been a premier landmark in Colorado Springs.*

Above: *"The Champ," a bronze of the legendary Casey Tibbs riding the famous bronc, "Necktie," greets visitors to the Pro Rodeo Hall of Fame in Colorado Springs.*

Right: *The Air Force Academy Chapel near Colorado Springs, shown here with a bronze of a B-24 bomber, is considered an architectural masterpiece. The building is the most visited man-made monument in Colorado.*

Above: *At 1,053 feet, the Royal Gorge Bridge is the world's highest suspension bridge.*

Right: *The neon lights of the casinos that line Bennett Street lend a festive air to Cripple Creek.*

Facing page: *Seven Falls leaps 181 feet in seven distinct steps.*

Left: *The colorful, eroded formations of Paint Mines State Park are a spectacular and entirely unique anomaly on the Calhan prairie in El Paso County.*

Above: *Big Stump in Florissant Fossil Beds National Monument is a beautiful example of a petrified ancient redwood stump from almost 35 million years ago.*

Right: *Sand cricket and kangaroo rat tracks intersect on a dune in Great Sand Dunes National Monument and Preserve, only to be swept away by the wind within hours.*

Below: *With Mt. Herard as a backdrop, Medano Creek flows before the massive dunes of Great Sand Dunes National Monument and Preserve.*

Left: *Sand dunes glisten on a frosty morning in Great Sand Dunes National Monument and Preserve, home to the most spectacular Sand Dunes in the Rocky Mountain West.*

Facing page: *As the sun rises, the reflection of Broken Hand Peak illuminates a pond in the Sangre De Cristo ("Blood of Christ") Mountains.*

Above: *Horn Peak, part of the Sangre De Cristo mountain range, rises above the golden aspens that have become synonymous with Colorado in autumn.*

Left: *Although they are seldom seen, bobcats roam craggy, dry mountains and foothills throughout Colorado. Photograph © Erwin & Peggy Bauer*

Facing page: *Parry primroses love water and can be found all over the Rockies in early summer.*

Above: *Sticky Geranium takes on a new dimension after a morning frost in the Sangre De Cristo Wilderness.*

Left: *Paintbrush and mountain blue bells in Rocky Mountain National Park glisten with the drops of a recent rainfall.*

Left: *Sangre De Cristo Mountains provide a pretty backdrop for an old barn in the Wet Mountain Valley.*

Above: *Young Ben Rusher lends a helping hand on a cattle drive in the Wet Mountain Valley.*

Right: *Flag bearer Sara Kettle shows the stars and stripes at the Westcliffe Stampede Rodeo.*

Below: *A saddle bronc rider tests his mettle at the Stampede Days Rodeo in Westcliffe.*

Facing page: *Cowgirl Donna Philips, cutting horse trainer extraordinaire, Pueblo.*

Facing page: *Music Mountain reflects the morning light in a pond near Upper Sand Creek Lake, Sangre De Cristo Wilderness.*

Above: *Waterfalls dance across the rock on Tijeras Peak, Sangre De Cristo Wilderness, San Isabel National Forest.*

Right: *Cowgirl Beverly Petrini shows how to swing a loop.*

Below: *Five-year-old cowpoke Matt Comerford ridin' herd.*

Facing page: *A rancher's hands reflect years of hard work.*

Left: *Kayakers practice on the stretch of the Arkansas River that runs through downtown Salida.*

Top: *Galleries line First Street in Salida, a small town well known for its art scene.*

Above: *Capricorn Sports in Salida shows off its toys.*

Hot air balloons brighten the skyline at Boulder Reservoir.

Above: *Sea kayaks add a touch of color to Frisco Marina on Dillon Reservoir.*

Left: *Where else but Summit County can you climb a fourteener and go sailing on the same day? Frisco's marina in the mountains is located on Dillon Reservoir.*

Above: *The Aspen Block Building, a fine example of Aspen's abundant historic architecture, was built in 1886 for $30,000, an exorbitant sum at the time.*

Right: *Aspen's Silver Queen gondola gets a much-needed rest during the summer months.*

Kids play at the Hyman Avenue Mall fountain in Aspen.

Facing page: *An old Model A Ford pickup perfectly accents a Lake County barn.*

Above: *The Maysville Schoolhouse held classes from 1882 until 1939, in Maysville near Monarch Pass.*

Facing page: *The ski resort town of Breckenridge has long been a popular winter destination.*

Above: *A skier jumps off a cornice at Monarch Ski Resort.*

Overleaf: *Vail's Bridge Street, with the Vista Bahn chairlift in the distance, assumes a festive glow as night falls. Vail is one of Colorado's premier ski resorts.*

Facing page: *You can almost hear dance hall echoes emanate from the shell of what was once the Blue Mirror Saloon (c. 1910), Ashcroft Ghost Town, near Aspen.*

Above: *The ruins of a general store and billiard hall amongst snowy windrifts in Caribou recall the extreme conditions miners braved to procure gold and silver in the 1880s.*

Left: *An old cabin in Ashcroft Ghost Town, left over from the silver mining boom, braves Colorado's legendary snowfalls in White River National Forest, near Aspen.*

Sopris Ranch looks tucked away for the winter beneath Mount Sopris in Pitkin County.

A couple takes a ride in a horse-drawn sleigh near Aspen.

Above: *This scene along Yampa Street suggests that spring has arrived in Steamboat Springs.*

Right: *Snowshoeing has grown tremendously popular in recent years. This enthusiast takes advantage of the ideal conditions on Rabbit Ears Pass, near Steamboat.*

Two women enjoy a sunny morning bike ride along a path in Steamboat.

The Colorado Columbine, Colorado's beautiful state flower, blends gracefully with the leaves of False Hellebore in Maroon Bells–Snowmass Wilderness.

Maroon Bells reflect vividly in Maroon Lake.

Above: *The black bear lives in the forests of central and western Colorado. Photograph © Erwin & Peggy Bauer*

Right: *The Old Mill at Crystal, also known as the Crystal Mill, was actually a hydro power generator for the Lost Horse Mill, which stood next to it along the Crystal River during Crystal's mining heydey.*

Colorado is a popular destination for mountain bikers worldwide. Here a couple navigates the Fence Line Trail in the Upper Cement Creek area, Gunnison National Forest.

Above: *Sunflowers in bloom dazzle a lush, green mountain glade beneath Bald Mountain in Gunnison National Forest.*

Left: *Sunflowers and lupine brighten the East River Valley in Gunnison National Forest.*

Facing page: *Mossy campion flourishes in the cracks of rocks, Maroon Bells–Snowmass Wilderness, White River National Forest.*

Left: *Dew clings to blades of grass on a cool morning, Maroon Lake, White River National Forest.*

Below: *Asters bloom near the base of an aspen tree near Aspen.*

Aspens in brilliant fall color provide a dramatic foreground for the Dallas Divide in the San Juan Mountains.

Flyfishing lures thousands of enthusiasts to Colorado's prime trout streams, including the Taylor River near Almont, each year.

Blooming fireweed adds a splash of color to a grassy meadow beneath Gothic Mountain, Gunnison National Forest.

Above: *Mule's ear, lupine, aster, and paintbrush set a hillside ablaze near Crested Butte.*

Facing page: *The Lake Fork of the Gunnison tumbles over rocks as it flows through the serene valley beneath Handies Peak in American Basin, Gunnison National Forest.*

Above: *The golden eagle, often spotted gliding through the skies over the Pawnee Grasslands, Rocky Mountain National Park, and Black Canyon of the Gunnison National Monument, has a wingspan of six to seven feet. Photograph © Erwin & Peggy Bauer*

Right: *Sunrise lights the rim of the Black Canyon in Black Canyon of the Gunnison National Monument.*

Overleaf: *Evening falls on the town of Crested Butte beneath Crested Butte Mountain.*

Elizabeth Becker rides a bike rigged with a ski rack, a common site in the skiing and mountain-biking mecca of Crested Butte.

Above: *The colorful storefronts of Elk Avenue lend charm and character to Crested Butte.*

Left: *On a snowy morning, a bicycle awaits its latte-laden rider at the "license plate building" near Camp Four Coffee, Crested Butte.*

Left: *Lake San Cristobal was formed more than 700 years ago when the Slumgullion Earthflow blocked the Lake Fork of the Gunnison River.*

Above: *Tourists admire the view of Lake San Cristobal, near Lake City.*

Above: *False front buildings line Silver Street in historic Lake City.*

Facing page: *Lake City is home to many historic buildings from its mining heyday, including the First Baptist Church, built in 1891.*

Facing page: *North Clear Creek Falls, located between Creede and Lake City in Rio Grande National Forest, is one of the more spectacular waterfalls in the Rockies.*

Above: *The Rio Grande River meanders on a foggy fall morning, near Creede, Rio Grande National Forest.*

The small town of Creede is famous for its annual repertory theatre festival, held in late summer.

Creede's main street is perhaps one of the most scenic and colorful of all of Colorado's old mining towns.

Wilson Peak provides an awe-inspiring backdrop for an old corral near Telluride.

The ski town of Telluride, shown here with Ajax Mountain, is known for its remarkable setting.

Left: *Young skiers take advantage of a sunny day and a fresh coating of powdery snow.*

Below: *Old sheep barns decorate a hillside near Telluride.*

Above: *Blue penstemon grows vigorously along an old fence near Telluride.*

Right: *A remnant of Colorado's colorful past, abandoned mine buildings and ghost towns, such as these buildings at Alta ghost town, Uncompahgre National Forest, near Telluride, can be found all over the Rockies.*

Red Mountain No. 1 reflects beautifully in a lake near Red Mountain Pass, not far from Ouray.

Columbine flourishes among the bluebells in a Colorado meadow.

Above: *Aspens reflect their fall splendor in a small lake near Telluride.*

Right: *An autumnal Uncompahgre Valley stretches for miles beneath the San Juan Mountains.*

Above: *The glasslike surface of Molas Lake in Uncompahgre National Forest captures a serene reflection of the mountains and sky above.*

Right: *Colorado is home to four species of fox—the red fox (shown here), the gray fox, the swift fox, and the kit fox. Photograph © Erwin & Peggy Bauer*

Facing page: *Paintbrush and sunflowers cover a hillside in Yankee Boy Basin, San Juan Mountains. During the summer months, the San Juans are home to an incredible variety of alpine and sub-alpine wildflowers.*

Right and below: *Sheer walls, deep canyons, and red rock monoliths dominate the landscape of beautiful Monument Canyon in Colorado National Monument.*

Left: *Harrison Yucca thrives in a patch of snow at Colorado National Monument. The Kissing Couple Monument stands in the distance.*

Top: *Named by an early traveler for a style of derby hat, Plug Hat Butte glows in the evening light.*

Above: *Fragile "goblin" formations mark the desert terrain of Bureau of Land Management (BLM) lands north of Grand Junction.*

Right: *The last rays of the day highlight the cliffs above Hunter Canyon in the Little Book Cliffs Area, BLM lands.*

Overleaf: *The centerpiece of Mesa Verde National Park, Cliff Palace is the largest and most magnificent of the many cliff dwellings found in the park. The ancestral Pueblo peoples built and lived in these dwellings around 1200–1300 A.D.*

Above: *The window openings of the "Beer Cellar" in Long House Ruins, Mesa Verde National Park, illustrate the attention to detail within the ancient Anasazi culture.*

Facing page: *The sun sets on Square Tower house, one of the many cliff dwellings found in Mesa Verde National Park.*

Lowry Pueblo, named after early homesteader George Lowry, is part of Canyons of the Ancients National Monument. The Pueblo, constructed by ancestral Pueblo peoples around 1060 A.D., was home to about a hundred people.